Stores & Retail Spaces 11

From the Retail Design Institute and the Editors of *VMSD* magazine

MEDIA GROUP

INTERNATIONAL

Cincinnati, Ohio

ISBN 10: 0-944094-66-X
ISBN 13: 978-0-944094-66-2

Published by:
ST Books, a division of ST Media Group International Inc.
11262 Cornell Park Drive / Cincinnati, Ohio 45242
P: 513-263-9399 / F: 513-744-6999 / E: books@stmediagroup.com
www.bookstore.stmediagroup.com

Distributed outside the U.S. to the book and art trade by:
Collins Design, an Imprint of HarperCollins Publishers
10 East 53rd Street / New York, NY 10022
www.harperdesigninternational.com

Cover and book designed by Kim Pegram, Senior Art Director, *VMSD*.
Book written by Matthew Hall, Online Editor, *VMSD* and *Hospitality Style*, except as otherwise credited (various editors from *VMSD*).
Book proofread and indexed by Kristen Sprague.

Printed in China
10 9 8 7 6 5 4 3 2 1

Stores & Retail Spaces 11

From the Retail Design Institute and the Editors of *VMSD* magazine

For 39 years, retailers, designers and architects from all over the world have entered their finest projects in the *VMSD* International Store Design Competition. Members of the Retail Design Institute (formerly the Institute of Store Planners) gathered to determine the best in retail design excellence from a variety of diverse submissions.

Here are those recognized winners from the *VMSD*/Retail Design Institute International Store Design Competition published in *VMSD* in February 2009.

Also included are a number of winners from the *VMSD* Retail Renovation Competition published in *VMSD* in September 2009.

Contents

The Retail Design Institute's
Annual International
Store Design Competition

The 2008 Store of the Year might seem a somewhat unusual choice, since, for starters, it's not a store at all. Asian Paints Colour Store in Mumbai was created as a place for Indian consumers to see paint choices and get inspired by the various colors available to them to recreate in their homes. But it's all inspiration and suggestion. There's no actual product sold in the store.

"Home decorating in India has been handled almost entirely by contractors," says KBS Anand, president of decorative business at Asian Paints. "The Indian DIY industry is only now beginning. We wanted to de-mystify the category, to make our customers feel like experts in color and home decor."

The design, by Fitch Worldwide's Singapore office, is intended to present products within lifestyle contexts. It's inspired by "holi," the Indian color festival in the spring, during which powder and water, colored by medicinal herbs, are sprayed into the air to

fight the viral fevers and colds associated with the changing climate.

Hundreds of LED lights are suspended in an arch over the store entrance, and when a shopper selects a color from one of the pedestals, an electronic pulse shoots across the store's façade. Motion sensors hidden within each pedestal send a pulse of the selected color up through the archway lights, creating constant color shifts throughout the whole storefront. The backdrop to many of the room sets is a "domino" wall, a rotating tri-graphic system that allows as many as three colors to be displayed. The panels rotate every 10 seconds, providing a dynamic

example of how color can affect space. This project also won an Innovation Award for its concept.

– Steve Kaufman

CLIENT / Asian Paints Ltd., Mumbai, India

DESIGN / Fitch, Singapore – Darren Watson, Steve Jepson and Mariana Manja, design team

GENERAL CONTRACTOR / JK Furnishers, Mumbai, India

LIGHTING / Lighting Systems Consultant, Mumbai, India; Lumiere Project Lighting, Mumbai, India; Color Kinetics, Hong Kong

TRI-GRAPHICS / Infina Engineering, Mumbai, India

GRAPHICS & COMMUNICATIONS /Grandmother India, Mumbai, India

PHOTOGRAPHY / Mark Moreve, London

be colour confident
colour and space

welcome

green
nature
generosity
harmony
vigor
youth

The four-level, 96,840-square-foot space in Jakarta seeks to blend the edgy ethos of U.K.-based retailer Harvey Nichols with the rich artisanship of the store's Indonesian environs. At the center of that strategy is a recurring design reference involving the fusion of the parang form (a royal batik pattern based on the movement of a sea wave) with British op art. Designers from Callison integrated that visual element into the store's fixtures and shelving, as well as into its front façade.

CLIENT / Harvey Nichols, London

ARCHITECT / Callison, Seattle – Doug Shaw, project manager; Andy Shaw, lead designer; Jessica Eaton, Jeany Kim, Kate Lee, Quinn Brant, design team

GENERAL CONTRACTOR / PT. Daya Indria Permai, Jakarta, Indonesia

OUTSIDE DESIGN CONSULTANTS / Lighting Design Alliance, Long Beach, Calif.

TEXTILES AND WALLCOVERINGS / Carnegie Fabrics, Rockville Centre, N.Y.; Timorous Beasties, Glasgow, Scotland; Cole & Son, London; Brewster Wall Covering Co., Randolph Mass.; Marcel Wanders, Amsterdam, Netherlands

PHOTOGRAPHY / Chris Eden, Callison, Seattle

Neiman Marcus / Lenox Square Mall, Atlanta

New or Completely Renovated Full-Line Department Store / Award of Merit

First opened in 1990, this three-level store underwent a recent top-to-bottom renovation that stretched over seven phases and 20-plus months – and also involved the addition of 50,000 square feet of space to the existing 153,000 square feet. Designers from Charles Sparks + Co. sought to reallocate space and realign product categories to maximize the store's productivity. In addition, they worked to infuse the space with a contemporary luxury feel associated with the Neiman Marcus brand. Artisan lighting, custom vitrines and expanses of crisp white space punctuated with hot citrus hues help engender an upscale vibe.

CLIENT / Neiman Marcus, Dallas – Wayne Hussey, senior vice president; Cliff Suen, vice president, properties development; Ignaz Gorischek, vice president, visual planning and store development; Victor Molaschi, senior project manager; Chris Lebamoff, director of store planning; Megan Theriot, designer

DESIGN / Charles Sparks + Co., Westchester, Ill. – Charles Sparks, president and ceo; Don Stone, executive vice president/account manger; David Koe, senior creative director; Stephen Prosser, account coordinator; Rachel Mikolajczyk, resource studio director

CARPET / Bentley Prince Street Inc., Chicago; Tandus Group, Chicago; Burtco Enterprise, Dalton, Ga.; Constantine Commercial, Chicago; Invision, Chicago; Mannington Commercial, Chicago; Unico, Dallas; Ombre, Evanston, Ill.

CARPET TILE / Tandus, Group, Chicago

CERAMIC TILE / Stone Source Midwest, Chicago; Surface Group Intl., Barrington, Ill.; Daltile, Elk Grove Village, Ill.; Brann Clay Products Co., Alsip, Ill.

FABRICS / Julie Werley, Dallas; Chippenhook, Dallas; C.W. Fifield Co. Inc., Hingham, Mass.; Knoll Textiles, Chicago; Nathan Chapin, Chicago; Spinney Beck, Chicago; Niermann Weeks, Chicago; Willow Tex, Davis Junction, Ill.; William Switzer, Chicago; Maharam, Chicago; Holly Hunt, Chicago; Ombre Ind., Evanston, Ill.; Donghia, Chicago; Textus, New York; Robert Allen Group, Chicago; Nierman Weeks, Chicago; Du Bois Fabrics, Oak Lawn, Ill.

FLOORING / Mannington Commercial, Chicago

GLASS / Twin City Creative Mirror, Burnsville, Minn.; Skyline Design, Chicago; Archetype Frameless Glass, Harrisburg, Pa.; McGrory Glass, Aston, Pa.

GLASS TILE / Mixed-Up Mosaics, New York

LIGHTING / Bartco, Huntington Beach, Calif.; Columbia, Greenville, S.C.; Design Lighting Group. Atlanta; Hera, Norcross, Ga.; IO Lighting, Vernon Hills, Ill.; Juno Lighting, Des Plaines, Ill.; Lightology, Chicago; Lightolier, Fall River, Mass.; Litelab, Buffalo, N.Y.; LSI Lighting, Cincinnati; Prescolite, Spartansburg, S.C.; RSA Lighting, Peachtree City, Ga.

PAINT AND LACQUER / Benjamin Moore, Montvale, N.J.; Sherwin Williams, Cleveland; Wolf Gordon/Scuffmaster, Chicago; Behr, Santa Ana, Calif.; Crescent Bronze Powder Co., Oshkosh, Wis.; Modern Masters, Sun Valley, Calif.

PLASTIC LAMINATE / Wilsonart, Evanston, Ill.; Lamin-Art, Schaumburg, Ill.; Nevamar, Chicago; Formica, Cincinnati; Pionite, Chicago; Parkwood Chicago, Wheeling, Ill.

STONE / Innovative Marble and Tile, Hauppauge, N.Y.; Surface Group Intl., Barrington, Ill.; Coverings Etc., Miami; Stone Source Midwest, Chicago

WALLCOVERINGS / Thybony, Chicago; Innovations, Chicago; Hirshfield's, Minneapolis; Donghia, Chicago; David Goldberg Designs, Long Island City, N.Y.; Maharam, Chicago; Koroseal Midwest, Schaumburg, Ill.; Wolf Gordon, Chicago; MDS Wallcoverings, Elk Grove Village, Ill.; Designtex, Chicago; Knoll Textiles, Chicago; Carnegie, Chicago; Callard and Associates, Chicago; Metro Wallcoverings, Schaumburg, Ill.; Brunswig & Fils, Chicago

WOOD FINISH / R.S. Bacon Veneer, Burr Ridge, Ill.; Brookside Veneer, Cranbury, N.J.

PHOTOGRAPHY / Charlie Mayer, Oak Park, Ill.

Barneys New York / Las Vegas

New or Completely Renovated Specialty Department Store / First Place and Innovation Award

The Barneys New York in Las Vegas fronts on Sin City's frenetic Strip. To create an attractive alternative to all the hubbub outside the store's doors, designers from Jeffrey Hutchison & Associates LLC sought to infuse the 81,000-square-foot space in the Palazzo complex with an oasis-like feel. The three-level store's color palette is light and warm, with desert overtones. Its materials mix features rich woods (including cerused oak, teak, anigre and wenge), luxurious metals (such as antique brass and darkened bronze) and flooring consisting of limestone in the women's departments on the first two floors and weathered walnut planking for the men's lines on the third. A sweeping spiral staircase serves as a central focal point for the space. The project also won an Innovation Award for its finishes.

CLIENT / Barneys New York, New York – David Mew, Matt Reed, Philippe Hum, Lisa Gianni, Lisa Goldman, project team

DESIGN / Jeffrey Hutchison & Associates LLC, New York – Jeffrey Hutchison, Luis Fernandez, Agnieszka Chromicz, Kaydee Kreitlow, Betse Ungemack, Jason Linde, project team

ARCHITECT / HKS Architects, Dallas

GENERAL CONTRACTOR / Venetian Development, Las Vegas

OUTSIDE DESIGN CONSULTANTS / John-Paul Philippe, New York (decorative artist); Schwinghammer Lighting, New York (lighting); R.G. Vanderweil Engineers, Las Vegas (MP engineer); MSA Engineering Consultants, Las Vegas (electrical engineer); Walter P. Moore, Houston (structural engineer)

DECORATIVE CEILINGS AND PORTALS / George M. Raymond Co., Las Vegas

EXTERIOR CURTAINWALL AND STOREFRONTS / Manhattan Curtain Wall Co., Kowloon, Hong Kong

LIGHTING / Targetti USA, Fort Lauderdale, Fla.

MILLWORK / Patella Woodworking, Boston; SuperL Sequoia, Monterey, Mass.

STONE FLOORS / Silver State Marble, Las Vegas

PHOTOGRAPHY / Adrian Wilson, New York

25

Olympic Shop at The Bay / Vancouver, B.C.

New Shop Within an Existing Full-Line or Specialty Department Store / First Place

This high-profile shop – 5000 square feet of space on the main floor of The Bay's store in downtown Vancouver – showcases merchandise for the 2010 Winter Olympics to be held in that city and its environs. The space's centerpiece, a flowing "tree" made of blue and white stretched fabric, is one of several organic designs incorporated into the space. Polished chrome and white lacquer millwork reinforce a winter theme, as do large lifestyle graphics depicting frosty scenes and igloo-shaped fitting room pods. For visual contrast, designers from The Bay's in-house team used accents of blue and green to represent the nearby ocean coast-line and forests.

DESIGN / The Bay – Hbc Store planning, Toronto – Richard Hamori, *general manager, store planning, design and construction;* Steve Liberty, *director, store planning and design;* Ted Wilson, *senior manager, design;* Domenica Casucci and Kris Lindner, *senior designers;* Rick Tapper, *senior manager, construction;* Jim Fiset, *manager, construction;* Bernie Nigalis, *senior manager, procurement;* Ken Lall, *manager, fixture procurement;* Denis Frenette, *director/ISM/visual-field;* Ana Fernandes, *creative design manager/visual*

GENERAL CONTRACTOR / Parkwood Construction, Burnaby, B.C.
CARPET TILE / Shaw Contract, Mississauga, Ont.
FIXTURES / JP Metal America, Montreal
LIGHTING / Litemore Distributors Ltd., Weston, Ont.
TREE/FEATURE 'S' WALLS / Eventscape, Toronto
PHOTOGRAPHY / Ed White Photographics, Vancouver, B.C.

Luggage Department at Macy's Herald Square / New York

New Shop Within an Existing Full-Line or Specialty Department Store / Award of Merit

Shoppers entering the updated luggage department at Macy's iconic flagship are transported into an environment designed to evoke a 1960s-era airport terminal – complete with two long luggage "runways" reminiscent of airport luggage conveyors, light gray walls, aisles of pale gray terrazzo tile with a metallic fleck, and lighting that includes two lines of staggered fluorescents that create a cloud-like effect and a Prussian blue ceiling studded with 44 retro globe lights. The rear perimeter wall of the 13,300-square-foot space features a series of linear lightboxes across its top bearing luggage and transit-inspired backlit imagery.

CLIENT / Macy's Corporate Services, New York – Amy Hanson, senior vice president, property development; Karen Maskey, divisional vice president and SPACE Store Design and Planning; James Sloss, operating vice president, SPACE Design; Andrew Brezina, operating vice president, SPACE Planning; Jim Kelly, director, SPACE Design; Ken Lay, manager, SPACE Design; Chris Moser, manager, SPACE Planning; AmyLaughead-Riese, SPACE Lighting Design; Elizabeth Hancock, designer, SPACE Store Design

Macy's East, New York – Jeremy Renna, vice president, capital projects; Christina Cappy, vice president, visual merchandising and store design

Macy's Home, New York – Coleen Miller, vice president, stores and merchandise planning; Victor Lewis, vice president, visual merchandising; Kathy Hoppins, director, store planning

DESIGN / TPG Architecture, New York – Alec Zaballero, design principal; Diana Revkin, studio director; Rayann Shums, project manager; Sungmin Han, designer; Wai Kit Yeow, project architect

GENERAL CONTRACTOR / Gilman Construction, Long Island City, N.Y.

CARPET / Karastan Contract, New York

FIXTURES / Modern Woodcrafts, Farmington, Conn.; Prestige Store Interiors, Toledo, Ohio

GLOBE LIGHTS / Shaper Lighting, Cincinnati, Ohio

ILLUMINATED CEILING / Newmat USA, West Babylon, N.Y.

TERRAZO TILE / Innovative Stone, Hauppauge, N.Y.

PHOTOGRAPHY / Mark LaRosa, Brooklyn, N.Y.

For its second store in Toronto, jewelry retailer EKO created a "hidden treasure" theme for its locale in the city's Yonge & Elgington district. To pique the interest of passersby, an all-glass façade reveals little about the merchandise inside, as the jewelry is housed in a curved series of angled vertical columns that line the walls. At the center of the sales floor is a display case/concealed cash-wrap. Natural wood flooring laminate adds warmth to the predominantly white space.

CLIENT / EKO Boutique, Toronto – Mina Yoon, founder

DESIGN / Dialogue 38 Inc., Toronto

GENERAL CONTRACTOR / Canson Building Ltd., Toronto

MECHANICAL ENGINEER / George Chan, Toronto

HVAC / Zonex, Toronto

FLOORING / Markham Flooring, Markham, Ont.; Torlys Laminate Flooring, Mississauga, Ont.

GLASS AND HARDWARE / C&H Glass & Windows, Toronto

LIGHTING / Cadalog Distributors, Toronto

MILLWORK / Bestway Millwork, Toronto

PAINT / Benjamin Moore, Montvale, N.J.

STONE AND TILES / Ciot Technica, Toronto; John Marble, Toronto

PHOTOGRAPHY / Eric Lau, Toronto

Via Spiga / New York

Specialty Store, Sales Area Under 1500 Square Feet / Award of Merit

Brown Shoe Co.'s Via Spiga footwear brand is named after a high-fashion shopping street in Milan. To re-create the feel of that thoroughfare in the Via Spiga flagship at Broome and Broadway in New York, designers from Fitzpatrick Intl. Group "brought the outside in," creating a streetscape within the confines of the space's narrow footprint. The store's walls are lined with a series of awnings sitting atop faux window displays of the retailer's shoes and accessories. The center of the space is home to a "piazza" that includes a fountain set in the middle of a circular stone flooring and bracketed on both sides with curving banquettes. The back is anchored by a large black-and-white photo of the store's namesake Italian street.

CLIENT / Brown Shoe Co., St. Louis – John Mazurk, senior vice president, specialty retailing; Peter Kelly, vice president, store planning and facilities management; Paul Schroeder, vice president, visual merchandising and concept development; Paul Cutlip, director of store planning

DESIGN / Fitzpatrick Intl. Group, Southampton, N.Y. – Jay Fitzpatrick, designer; Tiing Hie Lau, CAD design development and renderings; Haena Im, project decorator

OUTSIDE DESIGN CONSULTANTS / Store Lighting Systems, Great Neck, N.Y

ARCHITECT / FRCH Design Worldwide, Cincinnati

ARCHITECTURAL GLASS AND METAL / A&B Architectural Metal Corp., Astoria, N.Y.

AWNINGS AND SIGNAGES / Midtown Sign, Long Island City, N.Y.

BANQUETTES / Chairmasters, Bronx, N.Y.

CERAMIC TILE / Daltile, New York; Hastings, New York

DRAPERIES / Horizon Window Treatments, New York

FABRICS / Carnegie, Rockville Centre, N.Y.

FINISHES / Post Logic Studio, Brooklyn, N.Y.

FIXTURE PUCK SYSTEM / Marlite, Dover, Ohio

FLOORING / Tilequest, Depere, Wis.

FLOOR MATS / Mats Inc. Stoughton, Mass.

FOUNTAIN / Garden Fountains, Pennsburg, Pa.

LEATHER / Townsend Leather, Johnston, N.Y.

LIGHTING / City Lighting Products Co., St. Louis

MILLWORK / Classic Millwork Design, Webster, Mass.

PAINT / Benjamin Moore, Montvale, N.J.

SHOP WINDOW CURTAINS / Dazian Fabrics, Secaucus, N.J.; Carnegie, Rockville Centre, N.Y.

WALLCOVERINGS / Maharam, New York

WATERJET TILE CUTTING / Waters Edge, Burlington, Iowa

PHOTOGRAPHY / Whitney Cox, New York

American Greetings asked designers from Pompei A.D. to create a store that would shake up the greeting card business and differentiate it from its rival, Hallmark. The result of that request is the Paper*thread space, whose name reflects the intersection of greeting cards sold in the store and the thread of life that ties together families and friends. That interconnection is physically represented by the store's central organizing element, a ribbon-like wall clad in felt shingles that carries the majority of the store's cards and related merchandise.

CLIENT / American Greetings, Cleveland
DESIGN / Pompei A.D., New York
OUTSIDE DESIGN CONSULTANT / Sommer Electric Corp., Canton, Ohio (lighting)
FELT / Southerland Felt Co., Madison Heights, Mich.
FIXTURES / Fleetwood Fixtures, Chicago
PHOTOGRAPHY / Randhir Singh, New York

The T-Mobile Playground store is designed to up the fun factor for those seeking to buy personal technology products. To evoke a playground feel, designers from Callison used white vinyl seating, fuchsia-pink accent pieces and yellow laminate display tables. Bold signage was used to provide a clear product hierarchy and minimize clutter.

CLIENT / T-Mobile USA, Bellevue, Wash.

DESIGN / Callison, Seattle – Eric Lagerberg, principal-in-charge; Ron Singler, design principal; Cindi Kato, client and project manager, director; Christian Jochman, designers, associate principal; Nicole Bentley, interior designer; Josephine Wong, FF&E sourcing; Tom Rasnack Sr., project architect, associate principal; Vina Anderson and Judy Jeska, project architects; Cheryl Usnick, architectural staff; Crystal Inge and Joan Insel, brand, associate principals

OUTSIDE DESIGN CONSULTANTS / Lighting Design Alliance, Los Angeles

AREA RUGS / Unique Carpets Ltd., Riverside, Calif.

BENCH AND STOOLS / Aceray, Denver

CARPET / Masland Contract, Mobile, Ala.

CHAIRS / Keilhauer, Toronto

CHANDELIER AND PHONE DISPLAYS / Dillon Works, Mukilteo, Wash.

ENTRY MAT / Pacific Mat & Commercial Flooring, Kent, Wash.

FIXTURES / idX, Seattle

FLOORING / Prairie Shores Ltd., Pleasant Prairie, Wis.

GAMETABLE OTTOMANS / Kaas Tailored, Mukilteo, Wash.

LIGHTING / Villa Lighting, St. Louis

LOUNGE SEATING / Commercial Seating, San Jose, Calif.

MESSAGING, GRAPHICS AND INTERACTIVE CONTENT / Publicis, Seattle

SCREENS / 3Form, Salt Lake City

SIGNAGE / Priority Sign, Sheboygan, Wis.

PHOTOGRAPHY / Chris Eden, Callison, Seattle

Under Armour / Annapolis, Md.

Specialty Store, Sales Area 3001 to 5000 Square Feet / First Place

The athletic T-shirt hasn't been the same since Under Armour founder Kevin Plank debuted his apparel concept in 1996 – a shirt that regulates athletes' body temperatures and wicks perspiration off their skin. Since then, the company has expanded to offer sports accessories, shoes and mountain-climbing apparel. The company's first retail space, in Annapolis, Md., is a 3-D representation of the brand. Shoppers enter the 4500-square-foot store the way athletes enter a field – through a tunnel. Once inside, they're surrounded by audio and visual messaging promoting the product. The store's futuristic design, by FRCH Design Worldwide, is fronted by an imposing bronze statue of its brand ambassador, "Big E" (former pro football player Eric Ogbogu). Its décor is a mix of steel, black and silver and features a 120-inch rear-projection HD television screen.

– Lauren Mang

CLIENT / Under Armour, Baltimore – Chris Hufnagel, senior director, retail development; Jen Spaulding, director, retail execution; Scott Plank, senior, vp

DESIGN / FRCH Design Worldwide, Cincinnati – Steve McGowan, vp, managing creative director; Scott Rink, director/project manager; Terri Altenau, director/project manager; Abby Jahnigen, interior designer; Rob Rink, director; Ryan McNaley, job captain

GENERAL CONTRACTOR / Mackenzie Keck, Hackettstown, N.J.

OUTSIDE DESIGN CONSULTANTS / KLH Engineers, Columbus, Ohio (MEP engineer); Paul J. Ford and Co., Fort Thomas, Ky. (structural engineer)

CONCRETE COLORANT / LM Scofield Co., Douglasville, Ga.

FINISHES / Tiger Drylac Powdercoat, St. Charles, Ill.; Nass Fresco Finishes, Fox River Grove, Ill.

FIXTURES / Vulkane Industrial Arts, Cincinnati

FLOORING / Bolon Flooring, Ulricehamn, Sweden; Welling Inc., Cincinnati; BL Wilcox & Associates, Whittier, Calif.; EcoSurfaces, Lancaster, Pa.; Armstrong, Lancaster, Pa.

MATERIALS / 3 Form, Salt Lake City, Utah

MEDIA / PlayNetwork Inc., Redmond, Wash.

PAINT / Benjamin Moore, Canton, Ohio

STOREFRONT AND FIXTURES / The Concrete Design Studio, Dover, N.J.

WALL FINISH / Johnsonite, Cincinnati

PHOTOGRAPHY / Paul Aresu Photography, New York

After successfully opening a variety of concession sites within department stores throughout its home country of Korea, the high-end golf brand Elord decided to open a flagship store at Elord Hills, its new headquarters in Seoul. Working with Elord's in-house team, JHP Design worked to create a space that combined the science of golf with the height of fashion. The store's curvilinear white exterior is reminiscent of the sand bunkers found on golf courses. Visual references to the sport within the store include fixtures clad in golf bag leather and illuminated flag pins.

CLIENT / Elord, Seoul, Korea

DESIGN / JHP Design, London – Raj Wilkinson, Claire Downes, Martin Williams, design team

ARCHITECT AND GENERAL CONTRACTOR / Opus + Monsome, Seoul, Korea

SOFA / Tacchini Forniture, London

FLOOR TILES / Domus Tiles, Surrey, U.K.

UPHOLSTERY / Romo Fabrics, Nottinghamshire, U.K.

SOLID SURFACE-FIXTURES / Formica, Cincinnati

ACRYLICS-FIXTURES / Lucite Intl., Southampton, U.K.

PHOTOGRAPHY / Courtesy of Elord, Seoul, Korea

Kira Plastinina / New York

Specialty Store, Sales Area 5001 to 10,000 Square Feet / First Place and Innovation Award

Kira Plastinina, a teenaged, pink-obsessed socialite from Moscow, chose a 5900-square-foot space in New York's SoHo between Houston and Prince streets for her first U.S. store. "They saw it as, 'If you can make it here, then you can make it anywhere,' " says Ken Nisch, chairman of JGA, the Southfield, Mich.-based firm that helped create that space. "Kira's every girl, but she's the girl the shopper wants to be." To play up that differentiation, the store's design capitalizes on Plastinina's energized, feminine personality. Bits of the wealthy wunderkind's Russian lifestyle are on display, with nods toward luxury and opulence in chrome columns, gilded mirrors and baroque-inspired wallcoverings. But the concrete floors and pop-art carpet patterns hint at a more rebellious, punk-glam side. This project also won an Innovation Award for its visual merchandising.

– Lauren Mang

CLIENT / KP Fashion Co., Los Angeles – Robert Higgins, president; Chris Talbot, director of construction; Chad Christensen, visual merchandising manager; Laura Nichols, vp of stores

DESIGN / JGA, Southfield, Mich. – Ken Nisch, chairman; Kathi McWilliams, creative director; George Vojnovski, project manager

GENERAL CONTRACTOR / Tom Rectenwald Construction Inc., Harmony, Pa.

MECHANICAL AND ELECTRICAL ENGINEERS / M-Retail Engineering, Westerville, Ohio

LIGHTING / Regency Lighting, Van Nuys, Calif.; Times Square Lighting, Stony Point, N.Y.; Bartco Lighting Inc., Huntington Beach, Calif.; Janmar Lighting Inc., Covina, Calif.; MaxiLume, Montebello, Calif.; Simkar Corp., Philadelphia; Lightolier, Fall River, Mass.; Hèmèra Inc., Montreal; Royal Pacific Ltd., Albuquerque, N.M.; Exitronix, Phoenix, Ariz.

MANNEQUINS, CUSTOM DECORAIVES AND HANGERS / Universal Display & Design Inc., New York

PHOTOGRAPHY / Laszlo Regos Photography, Berkley, Mich.

DFS Galleria / Macao

Specialty Store, Sales Area Over 10,000 Square Feet / First Place and Innovation Award

This DFS Galleria is in the Cotai Strip, the Las Vegas-inspired entertainment zone in China's Macau gambling district. The 110,000-square-foot DFS space, created by rkd retail/iQ in The Shops at Four Seasons complex, offers an ultra-luxe ambiance that rivals anything found in its Western counterpart. The store's sophisticated materials palette includes stone, metallics, relief panels, fabrics and wood veneers. For ease of shopping, the sprawling space is subdivided into three major sections – luxury boutiques, cosmetics/fragrances and fine jewelry/watches/accessories – and also offers "palette cleansing" transition zones where patrons can enjoy showcased artwork. This project won an Innovation Award for store planning.

CLIENT / DFS Group LLC, Hong Kong
DESIGN / rkd retail/iQ, Bangkok, RKurt Durrant, principal
PHOTOGRAPHY / Hans Schlupp, Beijing

Borders / Ann Arbor, Mich.

Specialty Store, Sales Area Over 10,000 Square Feet / Award of Merit and Innovation Award

To move the Borders chain beyond being simply a seller of books, music and movies, designers from the retailer's in-house teamed with JGA to create a store environment that would serve as a "headquarters for knowledge and entertainment." In keeping with that ambitious goal, the 29,000-square-foot space features a "launch pad" at its entrance that features the latest releases; a "sprout" multimedia zone; and a large overhead oculus that's designed to draw shoppers into a variety of "destination zones," including travel, cooking and wellness. This project also won an Innovation Award for graphics.

CLIENT / Borders Group Inc., Ann Arbor, Mich. – Steve Davis, senior vice president, operations; Jill Lyon, vice president, store planning/construction/visual; Meghan Holefka, manager, strategic initiatives; Val Wahna, store design manager; Richard Ledbetter, director, visual presentation; Paul DeRaud, associate director, fixture production and installation; Lisa Smola-Hollo, senior manager, architecture and design; David Weisman, senior construction manager

DESIGN / JGA, Southfield, Mich. – Ken Nisch, chairman; Kathi McWilliams, creative director

ARCHITECT / URS Corp., Southfield, Mich.

GENERAL CONTRACTOR / Eden Enterprises, Carmel, Ind.

OUTSIDE CONSULTANTS

Illumination Concepts, Farmington Hills, Mich. (lighting design); TES Engineering, Westlake, Ohio (mechanical and electrical engineering)

FIXTURES / Huck Store Fixturing Co., Quincy, Ill.; Insight, Southlake, Texas; Triad, St. Louis

FLOORING / Boylu, Adair, Ga.

FURNITURE / Harter, Middlebury, Ind.; Mitchell Gold + Bob Williams, Taylorsville, N.C.

GRAPHICS/SIGNAGE / LSI, North Canton, Ohio; Foto 1, Ann Arbor, Mich.; Shaw & Slavsky, Detroit; Advance Print & Graphics, Ann Arbor, Mich.; Steve Frank Studios, Clinton Township, Mich.; Yesco, Las Vegas

LAMINATES / Nevamar, Shelton, Conn.; Abet Laminati, Englewood, N.J.; Formica, Cincinnati

LIGHTING / Targetti North America, Santa Ana, Calif.; Daybrite, Tupelo, Miss.; Elliptipar, West Haven, Conn.

PAINT / Sherwin Williams, Cleveland

POWDERCOATING / Tiger Drylac, St. Charles, Ill.; Rohm and Haas, Philadelphia; Protech, Parsippany, N.J.

SOLID SURFACES / Corian, Wilmington, Del.; Wilsonart Gibraltar, Temple, Texas

TILE / Dal Tile, Dallas

PHOTOGRAPHY / Laszlo Regos Photography, Berkley, Mich.

World Duty Free / London

Specialty Store, Sales Area Over 10,000 Square Feet / Award of Merit

This store is in Terminal 5 at London's Heathrow Airport, and is World Duty Free's fifth store within that complex. The centerpiece of the space is a high-tech art wall – a stacked set of video screens where the travel retailer and the luxury brands it represents can run promotional messages. The store is also home to the Bar 5, which World Duty Free created in partnership with premium drinks giant Diageo and features a color-changing chandelier.

CLIENT / World Duty Free, London

DESIGN AND ARCHITECT / JHP, London –Paul Jones, Raj Wilkinson, Steve Collis, Martin, design team

OUTSIDE DESIGN CONSULTANTS / Light Tecnica, London (lighting); E+M Tecnica, London (engineering)

GENERAL CONTRACTOR / Edmont, Swindon, U.K.

CONTRACTOR-SUNGLASSES/WATCHES/JEWELRY SECTIONS / EF Group, Hailsham, U.K.

FLOORING / Capital Marble, London

PHOTOGRAPHY /

REI / Round Rock, Texas

Large Format Specialty Store / First Place and Innovation Award

Recreational Equipment Inc. – known to the world as REI – has become identified with its commitment to the environment, mostly by building stores that are sustainable and energy-efficient. But for its new store in Round Rock, Texas, REI had a few missions beyond pushing the green envelope. One goal was to develop its brand in central Texas. Another was to test this two-story concept in new construction. A videotaped study of another REI store conducted by Envirosell Inc. showed that people often hesitated at the entrance, not sure where or even if they wanted to go farther into the store. So a key element of the Round Rock store design, produced by Gensler, is a decompression zone, a welcoming area just inside the entrance bathed in natural illumination. Throughout the rest of the interior, aisles are wide and visual presentations are inviting and interactive. Fixtures were designed and built in-house to be facilitate customer self-service. This project also won an Innovation Award for green design.

    – Steve Kaufman

CLIENT / REI, Kent, Wash.

DESIGN/ARCHITECT / Gensler, San Francisco

CERAMIC TILE / Daltile Corp., Dallas

LIGHTING / Moss Inc., Belfast, Maine; Graybar Electric, Seattle

FLOORING / Interface, Atlanta; Expanko, Parkesburg, Pa.

FURNITURE AND FIXTURES / Joslin Displays, Wilmington, Mass.; High Country Millwork, Longmont, Colo.; Haworth, Holland, Mich.; Numark, Bellevue, Wash.; Leader Mfg., Port Orchard, Wash.; MTI, Hillsboro, Ore.; REI Fixture Shop, Renton, Wash.

TUBULAR SKYLIGHTS / Solatube International Inc., Vista, Calif.

PHOTOGRAPHY / Paul Brokering Photography, Denver

COMMUNITY CENTER

SECOND FLOOR

KIDS / PLAY AREA

FOOTWEAR

FITTING ROOMS

MEN'S

RESTROOMS

WOMEN'S

SELECT YOUR COFFEE TABLE

INSPIRED LIVING

HOME IS WHERE LOVE CARE AND SENTIMENTAL
VALUES BEGINS. WE TAKE PRIDE IN MAKING
YOUR LIVING ROOM TAKE MOST PLEASURABLE
PLACE ON EAETH WITH OUR FINEST FURNITURE.

For its first freestanding store, the high-end furniture seller SB Design Square wound up in a space in Phuket with a long frontage on the adjoining street, but a relatively shallow depth. To make the best use of that rectangular footprint, designers from rkd retail/iQ created an open, atrium-like space at the center of the store, surrounded by a "racetrack" aisle pattern. To entice shoppers into exploring all corners of the three-level space, end-of-aisle focal walls were installed. White flooring and vertical surfaces provides a neutral backdrop for the colorful merchandise displays, which include a variety of room vignettes.

CLIENT / S.B. Furniture Industry Co. Ltd., Nonthaburi, Thailand

DESIGN AND ARCHITECT / rkd retail/iQ, Bangkok, RKurt Durrant, principal

GENERAL CONTRACTOR / Appart Co. Ltd., Bangkok

FLOORING / Royal Ceramic Industries, Bangkok; Thai Ceramic Co. Ltd., Bangkok

GRAPHICS AND SIGNAGE / VSP Signage, Bangkok

LAMINATES / Wilsonart Intl. (Thailand), Bangkok

LIGHTING / Lighting & Equipment Co.Ltd., Bangkok

PHOTOGRAPHY / Courtesy of rkd retail/iQ, Bangkok

G

Get New Ideas

What's New!

It's For The Birds. It's prime bird-watching season. The leaves are off the trees, the feeders are full. You're going to oke buying seed. . You don't have to buy expensive seed mixes or fancy suets to attract birds to your feeder. Heck, you don't even need a traditional feeder. Start recycling: supplement your seed habit and provide a bird smorgasbord with scraps and leftovers you have right now in your kitchen. Fruit fat, bread, grains and vegetables all are candidates.

To "reel" shoppers into this sportsman's paradise near Baton Route, La., Bass Pro Shop's in-house design team created a Cajun-style lodge structure – complete with rusted corrugated tin and aged lap siding – reminiscent of old mills and villages in the region. Highlights within this "experience-oriented retail environment" include cypress trees, Spanish moss, an alligator pond and a general store constructed using the traditional plaster-and-brick method.

CLIENT / Bass Pro Shops Inc., Springfield, Mo. – Tom Jowett, vice president, design and development; Sean Easter, vice president, construction; Mark Tuttle, director, architecture; George Carameros, director, merchandise presentations and imagery; Lenny Clark, senior technical designer; Chris Koenig, design support; Glennon Scheid, interior project manager; Dennis Gromer, project manager; Ron McCrae, quality assurance manager; Monica Matthias, interior project manager – fixtures and signage; Rick Collins, taxidermy; Ed Dinkins, vice president, merchandising; Pam Honeycutt, purchasing agent/design coordinator

ARCHITECT / Creative Ink, Springfield, Mo.

GENERAL CONTRACTOR / VCC, Irving, Texas

OUTSIDE DESIGN CONSULTANTS / SWT Design, St. Louis (landscape architect); Cost of Wisconsin, Jackson, Wis. (aquarium contractor); Marvin Levine, Lipan, Texas (imagery consultant); Brundege Studio, Rogersville, Mo. (design consultant); Smith Goth Engineers Inc., Springfield, Mo. (MPE engineers); R.B. Lewis Ltd., Richmond, Va. (consulting engineers); Best Restaurant Equipment & Design Inc., Columbus, Ohio (restaurant design)

BOOTHS / Creative Seating, Baxter Springs, Kan.

CARPET / Mohawk, Calhoun, Ga.; KL Installation, Dallas, Ga.

CERAMIC WALL TILE / Unique Tile, Nixa, Mo.

CHAIRS, BARS AND STOOLS / Bryan Ashley Intl., Pompano Beach, Fla.

CONCRETE / Bomanite of New Orleans, Inc., Saint Rose, La.; Walk on Art, Baton Rouge, La.

ELECTRICAL / All Star Electric, LaPlace, La.

FAUX FINISHES / American Wildlife Studios, Inc., Greenwell Springs, La.

FIXTURES, IRON WORK, CHANDELIERS / Bass Pro Fabrication Shops, Nixa, Mo.

FIXTURES / Lozier, St. Peters, Mo.; Our Country Home, Harlan, Ind.; ColorBrite, Cincinnati; TJ Hale & Co.; Menomonee Falls, Wis.; Rocky Creek, Stephenville, Texas

GRAPHIC MURALS / Craftsmen Industries, St. Charles, Mo.

HVAC AND PLUMBING / Bernhard Mechanical Contractors Inc., Baton Rouge, La.

IMAGERY FRAMING / PFI Artworks, Kansas City, Kan.

IMAGERY PRODUCTION / Bass Print Solutions, Springfield, Mo.; Design Image, Maryland Heights, Mo.; Mozaic, St. Louis

LATH AND PLASTER / Southern Stucco Inc., Baton Rouge, La.

MASONRY / Cajun Tower Masonry, Houston

MILLWORK / Duggan Contracting Corp., St. Peters, Mo.

MURALISTS / Bob Sopchick, York, Pa.; Chad Bryan, Atlanta; Biruta Hansen, Liverpool, Pa.; Doug Bolly, Apopka, Fla.

PAINTING / Specialty Construction LLC, Baton Rouge, La.

SIGNAGE / Garage Graphics, Springfield, Mo.; Summit Installations, Louisville, Ky.

SPECIALTY FABRICATORS / Gordon's Fabrications LLC, Springfield, Mo.

TABLES, BASES / Shelby Williams, St. Louis

PHOTOGRAPHY / John Stillman, Photo Dimension Inc., Hollywood, Fla.

Sit Down Restaurant / First Place (Tie)

This combined dining/live music venue seats up to 300 in a long and narrow space – measuring 200 feet long, 50 feet wide by 30 feet high. Stacked, L-shaped seating that offers clear views of the stage is available on all three levels within the space. The interior features bleached woods, white leather, blue velvet and shimmering metallics that designers from Baldauf Catton von Eckartsberg Architects say work together to create an "urban playhouse" vibe. The rear of the space is anchored by an open concrete staircase strategically positioned to maximize people-watching.

CLIENT / Anthology, San Diego

DESIGN / Baldauf Catton von Eckartsberg Architects, San Francisco

BAR TOP / Sensi Tile, Detroit

FABRICS / Anzea, Fort Worth, Texas; Carnegie, Rockville Centre, N.Y.; Knoll, East Greenville, Pa.; Maharam, New York; TDC, Los Angeles; Yoma Textiles, New York

FURNITURE / Inn Décor, Colton, Calif.; Sandler, Atlanta; Martin Brattrud, Gardena, Calif.

MILLWORK / Spectrum Oak, Orange, Calif.

PHOTOGRAPHY / Rien van Rijthoven Architecture Photography, San Francisco

Spring Rolls / Toronto

Sit-Down Restaurant / First Place (tie)

Since its founding in 1996, the Spring Rolls chain has opened a half dozen or so restaurants in and around Toronto. Its latest locale – in the Sheppard Centre mixed-use complex in the city's North York neighborhood – is a two-level affair that's infused with natural stained woods, white iridescent sheet and upholsteries and muted pink/gold-toned accents. The centerpiece of the 16-foot-tall lower level is a "10,000 Crane" chandelier made of translucent ivory Japanese origami paper, while the 9-foot-tall upper level features six mirrored anchoring columns. The restaurant's bar/lounge sports an edgier feel, thanks to heavy doses of sparkling glass, stone and plastics.

CLIENT / Spring Rolls, Toronto

DESIGN / Dialogue 38 Inc., Toronto – Bennett Lo, principal

GENERAL CONTRACTOR / Cont-Top Construction Ltd., Scarborough, Ont.

MECHANICAL ENGINEER / The Mitchell Partnership Inc., Toronto

HVAC / Citysheet Metal, Toronto; Zonex, Toronto

ACRYLICS / Octolam, Toronto; ACL Displayworks, Scarborough, Ont.

FABRICS / Designer Fabric Outlet, Toronto; Triden, Toronto; Rainbow Rainbow, Toronto

FURNITURE / BNT Designs, Toronto

GLASS AND HARDWARE / Kanada Glass & Windows, Toronto

LAMINATES / Willis Group Ltd., Burlington, Ont.

LIGHTING / Cadalog Distributors, Toronto

MILLWORK / Bestway Millwork, Toronto

PAINT / Benjamin Moore, Montvale, N.J.

PAPER / The Japanese Paper Place, Toronto

STONE AND TILE / Ciot Technica, Toronto; Stonetile, Toronto; John Marble, Toronto

PHOTOGRAPHY / Eric Lau, Toronto

Press Club / San Francisco

Specialty Food Shop / First Place and Innovation Award

This two-level wine-centered shop is in the Four Seasons Hotel in San Francisco, and offers what designers from Baldauf Catton von Eckartsberg Architects describe as "an urban reinterpretation" of the nearby Napa wine country. The 8200-square-foot space includes a street-level retail shop, where bottles from eight area wineries are showcased in custom metal storage racks with sloped-wood shelves, and a subterranean cellar with tasting bars and expanded display space for the wineries introduced upstairs. The shop's city/country ambiance is reinforced by a materials palette that includes cork, stainless steel, walnut wood and concrete. Oversized and sculptural decorative lights help unify the space. This project won an Innovation Award for lighting.

CLIENT / Press Club, San Francisco

DESIGN / Baldauf Catton von Eckartsberg Architects, San Francisco

OUTSIDE DESIGN CONSULTANTS / 100 Watt Network, San Francisco (lighting); Creative Mint, San Francisco (graphics); Florendipity Photography, San Rafael, Calif. (photography); CB Engineers, San Francisco (MEP); DeSimone, San Francisco (structural engineering)

BOTTLES / Encore Glass, Benicia, Calif.

CERAMIC TILE-BATHROOMS / EuroWest, San Francisco

CONCRETE BAR TOPS-RESTROOM SINKS / Sonoma Cast Stone, Sonoma, Calif.

FURNITURE / Dependable Furniture Mfg., San Leandro, Calif.; Brent Comber Originals Inc., North Vancouver, B.C.; Warisan, Los Angeles; Andreu World, Palo Alto, Calif.; ISA, San Francisco; Martin Brattrud, San Francisco

LIGHTING / 100 Watt Network, San Francisco

METAL / Eclipse Design, Petaluma, Calif.

MILLWORK / Planet Architectural Woodwork, San Francisco

UPHOLSTERY / Knoll, New York; Architex, Northbrook, Ill.; Arc/Com, Orangeburg, N.Y.; Maharam, New York

PHOTOGRAPHY / Sharon Risedorph Photography, San Francisco

Cellar 360 / San Francisco

Specialty Food Shop / Award of Merit

Another wine-oriented shop in San Francisco took the runner's-up award in this category. Cellar 360 is a showcase for Foster's Wine Estates (the 360 in the name references the fact that the company's wines come from 28 wineries around the world). The 6150-square-foot space is subdivided into a variety of zones, including a wine-tasting area, a small restaurant, a retail space and a demonstration kitchen/classroom. Helping unify the space is a sinuous overhead ceiling element that's embedded with more than 2000 recycled wine bottles back lit by LEDs. In deference to Cellar 360's location in the historic Woolen Mill Building on San Francisco's waterfront, Miroglio Architecture + Design worked with the Architectural Resources Group to retain several original elements within the space, including its columns, wood-plank flooring and brick walls.

CLIENT / Foster's Wine Estates, San Francisco
ARCHITECTURE/DESIGN / Miroglio Architecture + Design, Oakland, Calif.
ASSOCIATED HISTORIC ARCHITECT / Architectural Resources Group, San Francisco
GENERAL CONTRACTOR / Fine Line Group, San Francisco
FIXTURES / Trinity Engineering, Rohnert Park, Calif.
PHOTOGRAPHY / David Wakely, San Francisco

Olé Holiday Plaza / Shenzhen, China

Supermarket / First Place

Olé is an upscale supermarket chain in China. For this new prototype, design firm rkd retail/iQ sought to create a consistent merchandising/customer service template suitable for rollout. The 54,000-square-foot Shenzhen store, located in the lower level of a shopping center, is laid out to offer shoppers a variety of paths for circulating through the space and exposure to different merchandising touch points.

CLIENT / China Resources Vanguard, Shenzhen, China
DESIGN / rkd retail/iQ, Bangkok – RKurt Durrant, principal
PHOTGRAPHY / Pruk Dejkhamhaeng, Bangkok

EXCELLENT
CARROT

Carrots contain not only many vitamins but also rich minerals such as Ca, Ka, and Fe. Carotene can keep eyes and skin in good condition.

Roche Bros. Supermarkets / Westborough, Me.

Supermarket / Award of Merit

For its 18th store, the family owned Roche Bros. of Massachusetts wanted a space that would reflect the regional grocery chain's half century-plus of operations while also serving the needs of today's time-pressed consumers. The result is a New England market design concept that imagined Roche Bros. taking over a historic mill building populated by a series of indoor market vendors. In the produce department, for example, the grocer's in-house team partnered with FRCH Design Worldwide to utilize natural light and "hero" fixtures reminiscent of a market square, with the produce presented in market-themed galvanized buckets, baskets and wood-slate crates.

CLIENT / Roche Bros. Supermarkets Inc., Wellesley Hills, Mass. – Jay Roche and Richard Roche, owners; Paul McGillivray, vice president of sales and marketing; Arthur Ackles, director of marketing; Gary Pfeil, general manager; Richard Ordway, director of maintenance; David Stratos, director of construction; Jen Donehey, in-house illustrator

DESIGN / FRCH Design Worldwide, Cincinnati – Andrew McQuilkin, vice president, managing creative director; Young Rok Park, design director; Lis Diaz, senior interior designer; Mike Juras, senior graphic designer; Carol Osterbrock, senior resource designer; HeeSun Kim, design director; Nikki Dubois, Heather Storer and Holly Trucco, interior designers

PHOTOGRAPHY / Javier Jarrin, OMS Photography, Cincinnati

To create a retail experience that would appeal to today's tech savvy/eco-conscious college students, Miller Zell created an on-campus convenience store at Brandeis University that offers an abundance of healthy food selections and everyday essentials in a modern market setting. The Provisions on Demand (P.O.D.) space features energy-efficient indirect fluorescent lighting, a lightweight hanging perimeter signage system whose print panels are made of recycled styrene, resin cast-stone panels and a signature visual focal point featuring archival photography from the Brandeis campus. The store's components are modular, which means they can be used in a variety of campus locales, including student unions and food courts.

CLIENT / ARAMARK Higher Education, Philadelphia – Nala Royal, vice president, marketing; Mark Walker, associate vice president of convenience retailing; Steve Gordon, general manager, higher education services

DESIGN / Miller Zell Inc., Atlanta –Jim Matthews, corporate vice president, account executive; Paul Pizzini, vice president, design director; Jim Schrier, project director, environmental design; Paul Wolski, art director, brand identity development; Wright Bunch, design engineering; DeAnn Campbell, program manager

COOLERS / True Foodservice Equipment, O'Fallon Mo.

FIXTURES, GRAPHICS AND SURFACES / Miller Zell Inc., Atlanta

FLOORING / Centiva, Cincinnati

FOUNTAIN EQUIPMENT / Lancer, San Antonio

HOT FOOD MERCHANDISER / Atlantic Food Bars, Palm Beach Garden, Fla.

PAINT / Sherwin Williams, Boston

PHOTOGRAPHY / Creative Sources Photography Inc., Atlanta

105

Located in a large regional mall in suburban Sydney, Australia, Hello Happy sells Asian pastries and bread products. To attract shoppers, Otto Design Interiors sought to create a space that was unique and quirky. The result is a space that features an eclectic blend of traditional and current Asian motifs, including exposed recycled bricks, natural timbers, animated graphics and neon signage.

CLIENT / Hello Happy, North Ryde, Australia

DESIGN / Otto Design Interiors, Summer Hill, Australia

BRICK / Eco Group Bricks, Melbourne, Australia

CONCRETE TILE / Aeria, Sydney, Australia

FINISHES / Porters Paint, Sydney; Bristol, Villawood, Australia

SOLID TIMBER / Aus Timber Supplies, Sydney, Australia

TIMBER VENEER / Briggs Veneers, Wetherhill Park, Australia

PHOTOGRAPHY / Jamie Gray Photography, Sydney, Australia

Cineplex Entertainment wanted its SilverCity Oakville Cinema in suburban Toronto to be more than a movie theater. To meet its billing as "the ultimate entertainment destination," the 45,000-square-foot complex houses 12 state-of-the-art movie auditoriums; an upscale, six-lane bowling alley and billiards parlor; two bars; a "child-minding area" complete with kid-friendly crafts, computer games and movies; party rooms and a retail store. The theater's exterior features a ruby-red glass façade over its main entrance. Inside, designers from Watt Intl. used that same color in selected areas to visually unite the space.

CLIENT / Cineplex Entertainment, Toronto – Bill Tishler, vice president design and construction

DESIGN / Watt Intl., Toronto – Jean Paul Morresi, executive creative director, Paulis Ciskevicius, senior designer; John Shaver and Brian Bettencourt, creative directors; Kristina Ostian, interior designer; Vicky Chin, intermediate designer; Matt DeAbreu, director, illustration and design; Michael Claessens, illustrator; Shahla Mulji, account manager

ARCHITECT / Core Architects Inc., Toronto

GENERAL CONTRACTOR / Avcon Construction Inc., Toronto

OUTSIDE DESIGN CONSULTANTS / Lightbrigade Architectural Lighting Design, Toronto (lighting)

AUDIOVISUAL / Lightsound Intl., Toronto

FIXTURES AND MILLWORK / Formica Canada, Toronto

Chemetal, Toronto; Octopus Products, Toronto; CIOT (Caesar Stone), Toronto; Corian, Toronto; MMI Inc. Toronto

FLOORING / Olympia Tile, Toronto; Stone Tile, Toronto; Centura Floor and Wall Tile, Toronto; Vifloor Custom Carpet, Toronto; SMDS, Toronto; Shaw Contract Group, Toronto; Johnsonite, Toronto; Parterre, Unionville, Ont.; Lees, Unionville, Ont.

FURNITURE / ISA, Toronto

PAINT / Benjamin Moore, Toronto

SIGNAGE AND GRAPHICS / Knight Signs, Woodbridge, Ont.

WALLCOVERINGS AND MATERIALS / Daltile, Toronto; Metro Wallcoverings, Concord, Ont.; Tile Technics, Toronto; Levey Wallcoverings, Oakville, Ont.; Set, Toronto

PHOTOGRAPHY / Richard Johnson, Richard Johnson Photography Inc., Toronto

F acing increased competition within the
  Saudi wireless communications market,
Mobily wanted a retail environment that
would maintain its base of value-oriented
customers while also capturing a greater
share of the premium-price users. To help
accomplish those goals, designers from
Lippincott created a circular space whose
exterior is partially wrapped in glass, and
whose interior is segmented into a variety
of merchandising zones with interactive
product displays. Blue lighting adds visual
interest to the store, and integrates the
brand's signature color into fixture designs
and hanging signage.

CLIENT / Mobily, Jeddah, Saudi Arabia

DESIGN / Lippincott, New York – Randall Stone, senior
partner; Fabian Diaz, partner; Guil Mesquita, senior
associate; Sarah Harris, associate

PHOTOGRAPHY / Courtesy of Lippincott, New York

Verizon Communications / New York

Service Retailer / Award of Merit

To tout FiOS, Verizon Communications' fiberoptic-to-the-home broadband service, designers from the Gruskin Group created a store inspired by the 1982 sci-fi movie, "Tron," where the lead character finds himself digitized inside a computer mainframe. Customers can peruse the FiOS service's TV/Internet/telephone offerings at a trio of consultation stations, each visually punctuated by an overhead hoop containing a cylindrical strand of hanging metal that's bathed in red light, Verizon's brand color. Each station houses a large wall screen where Verizon sales consultants take shoppers through product demonstrations by punching instructions into a touchscreen.

CLIENT / Verizon Communications, New York– James Brevard, manager, channel development; John Mangan, team leader, construction services; Joseph Purdy, marketing consultant; Dawn Wachsteter, project manager; Michael Clement, senior staff consultant; Paul McGuire, regional marketing; Beverly Smart, visual merchandising; Daniel DuBravec, systems development

DESIGN, ARCHITECT AND INTERIOR GRAPHICS / Gruskin Group, Springfield, N.J. – Kenneth A. Gruskin, principal; Joel Shulman, principal, architecture division; Ed James, technical director, industrial design; Bob Lyons, director, marketing services; Francine Paragano, director, interior design; Brooke Robinson, associate; Jeff Barcan, director, creative services; Ross Kovelman- IT manager

GENERAL CONTRACTORS / Tishman Interiors, West Haven, N.Y.; Sugrue Contracting, Long Island City, N.Y.

ENGINEERING / Emtec, New York

CEILINGS / Armstrong-Armstrong World Industries, Lancaster, Pa.

FIXTURES / Bishop Millwork and Fixtures, Balsam Lake, Wis.

FLOORING / Milliken, LaGrange, Ga.; Alloc, New York

FURNITURE / Steelcase Inc., New York ; Dauphin Worldwide, New York

LIGHTING / Amerlux, Fairfield, N.J.; Omega Lighting, Tupelo, Miss.

PROPS AND DECORATIVES / Shimmer Screen, Mt Vernon, N.Y.

SIGNAGE / Strategic Signage Sourcing, Clifton Park, N.Y.

INTERIOR GRAPHICS INSTALLATION / Print Intl. New York

WALLCOVERINGS AND MATERIALS / Wolf Gordon, New York; Trikes, Dallas

PHOTOGRAPHY / Ken Gruskin, Springfield, N.J.

Cellular South / Ridgeland, Miss.

Service Retailer / Award of Merit

Cellular South, one of the nation's larg-est privately held wireless companies, wanted to create a bricks-and-mortar retail experience that mimicked navigating its newly redesigned web site. To accomplish that goal, the creative team at Interbrand Design Forum created a floor plan whose traffic flow replicates consumers' online navigation patterns. The store's entry is home to a greeting station that's flanked by a "manage my account" section for those with a specific task on one side and a "life-style station" equipped with 28 computer stations for online browsing/shopping at the Cellular South site on the other. The design theme for the 4000-square-foot space was "clear connections," which translated into the widespread use of transparent elements and textured walls.

CLIENT / Cellular South, Ridgeland, Miss. – John McGee, creative development manager

DESIGN / Interbrand Design Forum, Dayton, Ohio

CEILING / EPS Specialties Ltd. Inc., Cincinnati

FIXTURES / AdEx, Cincinnati

FLOORING / Scofield, Los Angeles; Armstrong World Industries, Lancaster, Pa.

GRAPHICS / KSK Color Labs, Troy, Mich.

LAMINATES / Pionite, Auburn, Maine; Wilsonart, Temple, Texas

PAINT / Benjamin Moore, Montvale, N.J.

TECHNOLOGY / Intava Corp., Bellevue, Wash.

WALL PANELS / Interlam, Claudville, Va.

PHOTOGRAPHY / Greg Campbell, Jackson, Miss.

smart **Showroom** / Davie, Fla.

Manufacturer's Showroom / Award of Merit

This U.S. dealership prototype for smart, the micro-car from the Mercedes Group, sports a minimalist theme throughout. The showroom's exterior is almost entirely black, while the interior is predominantly white. Splashes of the brand's signature yellow are incorporated into such features as the reception desk counter, a focal wall and fixtures that are shaped like the letter "r" in its logo.

CLIENT / smart USA, Bloomfield Hills, Mich. – Russ Hill, director, retail operations

DESIGN / Interbrand Design Forum, Dayton, Ohio – Scott Jeffrey, chief creative officer

CERAMIC TILE / Graniti Fiandre, Castellarano, Italy

FIXTURES / Ideal Image, Englewood, Ohio

FURNITURE / Steelcase, Grand Rapids, Mich.; Gordon Intl., New York; Metro, Oakland, Calif.

GRAPHICS / Innovative Media, Madison Heights, Mich.

LAMINATES / Pionite, Auburn, Maine; Lamicolor SpA, Englewood, N.J.

LIGHTING / Focal Point, Chicago; Lightolier, Fall River, Mass.; Ardee Lighting, Shelby, N.C.; Eureka Lighting, Montreal

SIGNAGE / Pattison, Toronto

WALLCOVERING / Genon, Fairlawn, Ohio

PHOTOGRAPHY / Jamie Padgett, Padgett & Co., Chicago

Look Fab Moments / Toronto

Temporary Store / First Place

Setting up shop for a three-week stint in a temporary storefront on Toronto's high-profile Bloor Street, the Look Fab Moments space offered consumers a chance to try P&G beauty products in three rooms housing four separate stations: essentials bar, skin boutique, color lounge and style salon. Designers from Upshot used rich paint colors, layered textures and vinyl wall designs to create an intimate, lounge-like setting. Plush pink cushions were scattered throughout the space for use by patrons awaiting their turns at the beauty stations.

CLIENT / Procter & Gamble Canada, Consumer Beauty Care, Toronto – Rob Linden, brand manager; Esther Benzie, associate marketing director; Stephanie Couture, assistant business manager

DESIGN, ARCHITECTURE AND LIGHTING / Upshot, Chicago – Brian Priest, vice president environmental design; Lisa Hurst, vice president account management; Stacie Thompson, senior art director; Brooke Ward, account manager

GENERAL CONTRACTOR AND FIXTURES / The Taylor Group, Brampton, Ont.

FLOORING / Forbo, Baar, Switzerland

LIGHTING / Le Klint, Odense, Denmark; Eurolite, Toronto; The Taylor Group, Brampton, Ont.; SIGNAGE / Signs by Tomorrow, Chicago

TECHNOLOGY / Izzy Design, Spring Lake, Mich.

PHOTOGRAPHY / Mark A. Steele, Columbus, Ohio

Andres Peller Ltd., a leading Canadian vintner, wanted to create a retail environment for grocery store locales that would appeal to both wine connoisseurs and casual customers. To fill that bill, designers from Perennial Inc. created Aisle 43 in a Zehrs Supermarket in St. Catharines, Ont. (the number reflects the latitude of the surrounding Niagara region). The wine is merchandised first by color and then by price, with each category marked by signage that runs atop the metro wire shelving. The white-and-bright space also sports a feature wall for new arrivals and promoted products where individual bottles are displayed in custom holders and a "Discover" station, which houses a self-serve wine-tasting machine.

CLIENT AND GENERAL CONTRACTOR / Andrew Peller Ltd., Grimsby, Ont. – Jim Cole, director of retail; Michelle Brisebois, marketing manager

DESIGN / Perennial Inc., Toronto – Marjorie Ogden, business director; Diane Mahony, director, client services; Kelley Doris, director, communications; Solange Rivard, creative director, graphics; Tara O'Neil, chief creative officer; Mardi Najafi, senior designer, environments

AUDIO/VISUAL / Splash Interactive, Toronto

FLOORING / Fritz Industries Inc., Mesquite, Texas

WINE DISPENSER / Winegate Solutions, Montreal

PHOTOGRAPHY / Richard Johnson, Toronto

reds

$10 – $15   under $10

Zonic / Jeddah, Saudi Arabia

Innovation Award for Fixture Design

This colorful and kinetic retail space sells high-end consumer electronics to tech-savvy shoppers in the Al Sayrafi Mall in Saudi Arabia. The store features several custom "demo-go-round" kiosks, in which products are displayed on spinning wheels that rotate 360 degrees. All the gadgets on display are operational, giving customers a hands-on chance to experience their capabilities. Motion-activated LED lighting, hand-made art glass, terrazzo flooring and polished stainless-steel accents add to the slick, futuristic vibe.

CLIENT / Zonic, Khobar, Saudi Arabia

DESIGN, FIXTURES, DISPLAYS, INTERACTIVE MERCHANDISING SYSTEMS, SIGNAGE AND GRAPHICS / Winntech, Kansas City, Mo. – Barrett Prelogar, senior principal; Steve Owens, chief technology officer; Dave Onkels, digital and online content director; Franco Cagnina, industrial design director; Jon Price, industrial design, level II; Chris Vogel, art director; Gretchen Townsend, production artist; Roger Ngo, electrical engineering, hardware and software development; J.J. Pieschl, production engineering director; Steve Klein, head digital animator; Jeff Woods and Ed Reed, production engineers

OUTSIDE DESIGN CONSULTANTS / Lippincott, New York (brand development)

ARCHITECTURAL CONSULTING / Nearing, Staats, Prelogar and Jones Architects, Prairie Village, Kan.

MEP ENGINEERING CONSULANT / Larson Binkley Engineering, Overland Park, Kan.

GENERAL CONTRACTOR / United Electronics Corp., Jeddah, Saudi Arabia

LIGHTING / Journee Lighting Inc., Westlake Village, Calif.; Foley Group Inc., Kansas City, Kan.; Philips Color Kinetics, Burlington, Mass.; Contrasl Lighting, Saint-Jean-Chrysostome, Que.

PHOTOGRAPHY / Muhammad Janhangeer Kokar, Jeddah, Saudi Arabia

This 10,000-square-foot showroom/office space seeks to put a future-oriented spin on Timberland's roots as an eco-friendly designer/marketer of footwear, apparel and accessories for outdoor enthusiasts. Designers from Cubellis Inc. brought a variety of outdoor elements into the space, including trees made of stainless steel with carved branches inspired by Timberland's logo at the entrance. The interior features flooring accents incorporating river rocks and ashwood wall panels. The space is illuminated with natural lighting and energy-efficient LEDs.

CLIENT / Phillips-Van Heusen, New York – Doug Jankowski

DESIGN / Cubellis Inc., New York – David Rush, principal; Adam Snyder, senior project manager; Annie Lee, senior project designer; Russell Conley, senior job captain

OUTSIDE DESIGN CONSULTANTS / WB Wood, New York (furniture); ZeroLUX, New York (lighting)

GENERAL CONTRACTOR / Americon Construction, New York

ENGINEER / Robert Director, New York

CARPETING / Interface, Atlanta

ELEVATOR DOOR FINISH / Wolf Gordon, New York

FURNITURE / Herman Miller, Zeeland, Mich.; Bernhardt, Lenoir, N.C.; Steelcase, Grand Rapids, Mich.; SofaRoche Bobois, New York; Troy, New York; Urban Office, New York; ALEA, New York; Peter Mann, New York

PANTRY BACKSPLASH TILE / Stone Source, New York

RESIN WALLS / 3Form, Salt Lake City

RIVER ROCK PEBBLES / Miami Beach Pebbles, Miami

SHOWROOM DISPLAYS / B&N Industries, Burlingame, Calif.

TACKBOARD PANELS / Knoll Fabric, New York

UPHOLSTERED WALL / Maharam, New York

WALL FINISHES / DFB, New York

WALL SYSTEMS / DIRTT, New York

PHOTOGRAPHY / Eric Laignel, New York

The *VMSD* Retail
Renovation Competition

Ermenegildo Zegna flagship / New York

Retail Renovation of the Year

The Cinderella-style reimaging of Ermene-gildo Zegna Group's Fifth Avenue mens-wear store as its first U.S. flagship sums up the "do's" of retail renovation. It's creative; it's subtle; it's a sales-booster and it's all about the brand.

Peter Marino Architect gave a nod to Zegna's heritage and its Italian roots with the yellow marble floor-to-wall stripe that references the selvage on its fabrics. But the designers also played up the brands' contemporary flare with industrial-cool stainless steel cables to simulate warp and weft, hand-sewn leather accents and warm masculine woods. More than 80 different materials were used to tell Zegna's story and define three distinct retail zones.

Vertical retailing amps up the store's visual merchandising power. Shawmut Design and Construction gutted the 100-year-old

building's interiors, enlarging the pre-existing 6000 square feet of selling space by more than 50 percent and creating a 22-foot-high glass entryway. Merchandise was pushed to the front of all three floors to tempt passersby. "It has to be obvious that great things exist on every floor," says Les Hiscoe, vice president, retail, Shawmut Design and Construction.

Nothing is accidental in the design, says Anna Zegna, image director. "Retail design is changing. It must tell a story, but it's more understated, more real. Customers don't want to be distanced by store design," she says.

– Mary Scoviak

CLIENT / Ermenegildo Zegna Group, New York City/ Milan

ARCHITECT/DESIGN / Peter Marino Architect, New York

GENERAL CONTRACTOR / Shawmut Design and Construction, Boston

LIGHTING DESIGNER / Metis Lighting S.R.L., Milan

LIGHTING SUPPLIER / LiteLab Corp., Buffalo, N.Y.

MILLWORK/FIXTURES / Cassina S.p.A., Milan

FLOORING / Haywood-Berk Floor Co., Inc., New York

'AFTER' PHOTOGRAPHY / Paul Warchol, New York

Dollar Bank / Cleveland

Service Retailer / First Place

Although Dollar Bank had a presence in Cleveland for more than two decades, the bank's history of second-tier locations gave it a low profile. A failed downtown mall offered the solution to its location issues, but the bank still had to develop an image that would convey solidity in a climate that's anything but.

Eberhard Architects (formerly Oliver Design Group Architects) found the visual heart of the new brand image in the two stone lions that guard the entrance of Dollar Bank's main branch in Pittsburgh. Looking through the glass envelope that wraps the bank, its customers can't help but see the two-story image of a lion that dominates the lobby. Nor can they miss the plasma screen message that combines the bank's logo with the comforting words "since 1855."

Sustainability and fresh colors lighten up the public spaces, says William Eberhard, the firm's founder. Even the private banking areas keep the mood fresh, borrowing the same materials from the lobby and adding a bit more wood. The firm played up the reflective quality of porcelain tiles and luminous glass films for a look that balances transparency and privacy.

– Mary Scoviak

CLIENT / Dollar Bank, Cleveland

ARCHITECT/DESIGN/LIGHTING DESIGN / Eberhard Architects, Cleveland

FIXTURES / Formica Corp., Cincinnati (laminate); Nevamar, Odenton, Md. (laminate); Lamin-Art, Schaumburg, Ill. (laminate); Wilsonart Intl., Temple, Texas (laminate); Corian (DuPont), Wilmington, Del. (solid surface) ; LG Surfaces, Peoria, Az. (solid surface)

FLOORING / Shaw Industries, Dalton, Ga. (carpet); J&J Industries, Dalton, Ga. (carpet); Atlas Carpet Mills, Los Angeles (carpet); Lees, Greensboro, N.C. (carpet); Walker Zanger, Sylmar, Calif. (tile); Impronta Italgraniti U.S.A Inc., Springfield, Va. (tile); StonePeak, Chicago (tile); Armstrong, Lancaster, Pa. (resilient)

GLASS / Oldcastle Glass, Santa Monica, Calif.

GLASS MOSAIC TILE / Bisazza, Miami

MOTORIZED SHADES / Albert Herman Draperies, Cleveland

WALLCOVERINGS / D.L. Couch, New Castle, Ind.; Sanfoot, St. Ouen, France; Vescom, Henderson, N.C.; Sherwin-Williams, Cleveland (paint)

FURNITURE / Haworth, Holland, Mich. (systems furniture, task seating, conference tables, files); HBF, Hickory, N.C. (conference seating, occasional tables); Source International, Shrewsbury, Mass. (training seating); Nucraft, Comstock Park, Mich. (training tables); Keilhauer, Toronto (lounge seating); David Edwards, Baltimore (lounge seating); Carolina Business Furniture, Archdale, N.C. (lounge seating); Davis, High Point, N.C. (lounge seating, café tables); Krug, Kitchener, Ont. (guest chairs); Martin Brattrud, Gardena, Calif. (banquet seating); Allermuir, Saint-Georges, Qué.(lunchroom seating); Egan, Woodbridge, Ont. (white boards); Peter Pepper Products Compton, Calif. (waste and recycling receptacles)

LIGHTING / Spectrum, Fall River, Mass.; Zumtobel, Highland, N.Y.; Lithonia, Lithonia, Ga.; Kirlin, Detroit; Focal Point, Chicago; Belfer, New York; Alkco, Franklin Park, Ill.; Progress, Greenville, S.C.; Translite Sonoma, Shelby, N.C.; Bega, Carpentaria, Calif.; Kim, City of Industry, Calif.; Gotham, Conyers, Ga.; Lightology, Chicago; Energie, Golden, Colo.; Omega, Tupelo, Miss; Con-Tech, Northbrook, Ill.

'AFTER' PHOTOGRAPHY / Dan Cunningham, Arlington, Va.

Brown University Bookstore was studying ways to expand its appeal to both students and the broader market living within its College Hill Community. But display cases filled with Brown memorabilia, stacks of text books and fixtures that obstructed the windows weren't making the grade.

Borrowing a little third-place attitude, designer Bergmeyer Associates moved racks of best-sellers and a café toward the main entrance. Cozy niches invite shoppers to relax between the stacks or be more social in the open-plan café. A new home for the cashwrap and display cases uncovered the windows, filling both the first floor and upper level with natural light.

Since most textbooks are hot buys only twice a year, they were relocated from the mezzanine to the basement. That freed up prime estate real for positioning the computer store from the lower level to visual prominence. For added retail punch on the mezzanine, the designers created "Your Space" filled with furniture, household items, sundries and design ideas for dorms and apartments. Apparel came off crowded racks to be hung on wall fixtures or folded on tables where it could be cross-merchandised with other products.

– Mary Scoviak

CLIENT / Brown University, Providence, R.I.

ARCHITECT/DESIGN / Bergmeyer Assoc., Inc., Boston – Joseph P. Nevin, Jr., principal; Mare Weiss, associate; Dan Broggi, senior project architect; Mai Nguyen, interior designer; Anna Butterfield, job captain

GENERAL CONTRACTOR / Suffolk Construction, Boston

OUTSIDE DESIGN CONSULTANTS / Lighting Collaborative, Concord, Mass.; Monarch Industries, Warren, R.I.

FURNITURE / Malik Gallery, Oakland, Calif.; Allermuir Ltd., Darwen, Lancashire, U.K.; Thonet, St. Louis; Bernhardt, Boston; Brayton International, High Point, N.C.; Prismatique, Toronto; West Coast Industries, San Francisco

FABRICS / Sina Pearson, New York; Designtex, Boston; Arc-Com, Boston; HBF Textiles, Hickory, N.C.; Knoll Studio, Boston; Architex, Boston

PAINT / Benjamin Moore, Montvale, N.J.

FLOORING / Armstrong, Lancaster, Pa.; Milliken, LaGrange, Ga.; Atlas, Los Angeles; Mirage, Saint-Georges, Qué.; Mannington, Salem, N.J.

'AFTER' PHOTOGRAPHY / Warren Jagger, Providence, R.I.

GUESS? Michigan Avenue / Chicago

Specialty Store, Sales Area Over 10,000 Square Feet / Honorable Mention

It took just four days and one-third of the typical renovation budget to transform the GUESS? store on Chicago's Magnificent Mile from warm and woodsy to modern and minimalist. The secret? Reusing and repurposing as many of the existing design elements as possible.

Maple floor and perimeter fixtures were updated with an environmentally friendly coating of "Super White." "The white backdrop serves as a canvas that can be transformed easily with new trends, campaigns and brand directives," says Vember Stuart-Lilley, Guess? Inc.'s special projects manager, retail development.

The brand's signature denim clothing pops against the pristine background. Strategic use of black-and-white patterned wall treatments draws attention to the shop-in-a-shop accessories department. "It's imperative that we have a living retail space that is modular and easy to re-image within a limited time frame and budget," says Stuart-Lilley. That approach gave new life to 95 percent of the store's floor and perimeter fixtures while building its bottom line with a recession-busting increase in foot traffic.

– Mary Scoviak

CLIENT / Guess?, Inc., Los Angeles

ARCHITECT / McCall Design, San Francisco – David Lew, vp

DESIGN / Guess?, Inc. – Vember Stuart-Lilley, special projects manager; Albert Morales, project manager; Lisa Myers, senior purchasing project coordinator

GENERAL CONTRACTOR / Davaco Inc., Dallas

ISP PAINTING / Interior Painting (ProBond), Naperville, Ill.

COATING MATERIAL / ProCoat Products (ProBond), Holbrook, Mass.

WINDOW DISPLAY / B+N Industries, Burlingame, Calif.

FIXTURES / Hamilton Fixture, Ontario, Calif.

FURNITURE / Room Service, Los Angeles; Blue Print, Los Angeles

WALLCOVERING / Osborne & Little, Los Angeles

RUGS / Sansom Shag Rugs, Dalton, Ga.

PHOTOGRAPHY / Courtesy of Guess? Inc., Los Angeles

Sinn Leffers / Bielfeld, Germany

Specialty Store, Sales Area Over 10,000 Square Feet / Honorable Mention

B efore, Sinn Leffers' Bielfeld location was a grid of stacks and racks framed by a big expanse of beige. Pleasantly shoppable? Certainly. But predictable good looks fell short of the wow factor the group's leadership wanted in this 91,500-square-foot department store. To support the brand, Sinn Leffers mandated a complete visual redirection—from the architecture and design down to the logo and graphics.

Designer Schwitzke & Partner colorcoded the three-level store to create easily identifiable destinations. Dark tones add drama to menswear and women's designer fashions on display on the lowest floor. Though the black-and-white theme carries through the entire store, the mood lightens

and brightens on the main floor and second level thanks to changes in lighting and the impact of reflective surfaces.

A high materials mix delivers an edgy feel. Polished steel contrasts with different varieties of wood, brown lacquered glass, leather and glossy black. To keep the space uncluttered but interesting, essentials become art. Decorating the walls are lambskin panels, wallpaper tailored to each fashion theme and "wall tattoos." Even the lighting adds attitude, from long lines of black track lighting to black backgrounds for sparkling recessed spotlights.

– Mary Scoviak

CLIENT/RETAIL DESIGN / Sinn Leffers GmbH, Hagen, Germany

ARCHITECT/DESIGN / Schwitzke & Partner, GmbH, Düsseldorf – Karl Schwitzke, managing partner; Richard Wörösch, general manager

GENERAL CONTRACTOR / Schwitzke Project GmbH, Düsseldorf, Germany

LIGHTING / Ansorg BeluxGmbh, Mülheim an der Ruhr, Germany

SHOPFITTING / Korda Ladenbau GmbH, Bad Salzuflen, Germany

'AFTER' PHOTOGRAPHY / Oliver Tjaden, Düsseldorf

When shoppers entered Douglas Parfumerie prior to its renovation, they were greeted with products shelved chock-a-block in displays that ranged the perimeter walls and sprouted up haphazardly in the middle of the selling area. The aim of the renovation was not only to bring order to the nearly 5000-square-foot store, but also to create the ambiance of an emporium that features distinct brands at different price points.

The redesign began by envisioning the store as four rooms, each opening onto the next. Doorway arches crafted from black-lacquered wood mark the end of one experience and the beginning of the next. Each room has its own atmosphere, defined by signature wall coverings and fixtures. Color is also an identifier. Black accents set a luxurious tone in the first room. Deep purples start the change to a different mood. Golden wood tones keep the ambiance glowing until shoppers enter the modern white showcase in the final area.

For a lifestyle touch, seating areas invite customers to linger a bit. Even the cashwrap has the feel of a check-in desk at a posh hotel.

– Mary Scoviak

CLIENT/RETAIL DESIGN / Parfümerie Douglas Deutschland GmbH, Hagen, Germany

ARCHITECT/DESIGN / Schwitzke & Partner GmbH, Düsseldorf – Karl Schwitzke, managing partner; Richard Wörösch, general manager

GENERAL CONTRACTOR / Köster Ladenbau, Hagen, Germany

LIGHTING / Ansorg BeluxGmbH, Mülheim an der Ruhr, Germany

'AFTER' PHOTOGRAPHY / Markus Kratz, Düsseldorf

The North Face / Boise, Idaho

Specialty Store, Sales Area Under 10,000 Square Feet / Honorable Mention

The North Face wanted its environmental commitment to be more than window dressing for its new store in Boise. So instead of clear-cutting a suburban site, the outdoor clothing and equipment retailer repurposed a downtown department store that had been shuttered since 1991.

Retail designer and branding firm JGA prioritized recycling and reuse of existing materials throughout the demolition and renovation of the 19th century building. Layers of modernization were stripped away to reveal the original joist ceilings, brick walls, cast iron rivets, metal beams and perimeter columns. Second floor windows, boarded up since 1958, were restored with high-efficiency glazing.

Since most of the merchandise is on display on the second floor, the designers needed to find a way to inspire shoppers to make the climb. The massive escalators in use when the store was subdivided into two retail spaces were replaced with a welcoming atrium staircase. The hard-to-ignore focal point alongside it is a large graphic mural and dramatic footwear wall which helps customers experience the rugged outdoors in the city center.

– Mary Scoviak

CLIENT / VF Outdoor Inc., San Leandro, Calif. – Lindsay Rice, vp, direct to consumer; Bernie Bishop, director of operations; Eric Green, director of visual merchandising; Rich Marini, director of stores

DESIGN / JGA, Southfield, Mich. – Ken Nisch, chairman; Mike Curtis, creative director; George Vojnovski, project manager

GENERAL CONTRACTOR / ESI (Engineered Structures, Inc.), Boise, Idaho

OUTSIDE DESIGN CONSULTANTS / M-Retail Engineering, Westerville, Ohio (mechanical/electrical engineering)
Lighting Management, Harriman, N.Y. (lighting)

CARPET / Interface, LaGrange, Ga.

WOOD WALL FEATURE / Junkers Solid Hardwood Flooring, New York

ENTRY MAT / Roppe, Fostoria, Ohio

FIXTURES / The Carlson Group Inc., Portland, Ore. ; Smith & Fong Co., Neptune, N.J.

LIGHTING / Zumtobel, Highland, N.Y.

SIGNAGE / Brite Lite Neon Corp., N. Hollywood, Calif.

MILLWORK / The Carlson Group Inc., Portland, Ore.

PAINT / Benjamin Moore Paints, Montvale, N.J.

ARCHITECTURAL ELEMENTS / Alpolic, Chesapeake, Va.; USG Durock Cement Board, Chicago

PORCELAIN TILE / Beaver Tile and Stone, Farmington Hills, Mich.

'AFTER' PHOTOGRAPHY / Laszlo Regos Photography, Berkley, Mich.

Ludwig beck Classical Music and Jazz Department / Munich, Germany

Specialty Stores, Sales Area Under 10,000 Square Feet / First Place

Ludwig Beck was registering a bit of dissonance between what the CD department in its Marienplatz store offered and what its customers wanted. The Munich fashion house challenged designer Schwitzke & Partner to build out the existing space and broaden the music section's appeal. "The intent was to give the department all the flare of a concert hall—not just a place to buy or sample music, but also to listen to CDs from beginning to end," says Richard Wörösch, managing director, Schwitzke & Partner.

Rethinking retail as lifestyle started by thinking like a music lover. The walnut-paneled walls have no right angles, allowing for better acoustics as sound flows along their rounded lines. Changes in design and materials help market the difference between, say, jazz and classical CDs or rock and world music. So the central furnishings in the classical music area feature dark woods and polished brass while the jazz

and world music sections are kept to simple blacks and whites. Photos add a humanizing vibe, offering shoppers shots of jazz greats to contemplate while they're tuned in. Shoppers can linger at the polished stainless steel listening stations, enjoying tracks from beginning to end.

– Mary Scoviak

CLIENT / Ludwig Beck AG, Munich

ARCHITECT/DESIGN / Schwitzke & Partner GmbH, Düsseldorf – Karl Schwitzke, managing partner; Richard Wörösch, general manager

LIGHTING / Ansorg Belux GmbH, Mülheim an der Ruhr, Germany

SHOPFITTING / von Bergh, Dernbach, Germany

PHOTOGRAPHER / Oliver Tjaden, Düsseldorf

For more information on visual merchandising and store design, subscribe to:

vmsd. Experience Retail Now

**Books on visual merchandising and store design
available from ST Media Group International:**

Aesthetics of Merchandising Presentation
Budget Guide to Retail Store Planning & Design
Complete Guide to Effective Jewelry Store Display
Feng Shui for Retailers
Green Retail Design
Retail Renovation
Retail Store Planning & Design Manual
Stores and Retail Spaces
Visual Merchandising
Visual Merchandising and Store Design Workbook

**To subscribe, order books or request a complete catalog
of related books and magazines, please contact:**

**MEDIA
GROUP**
INTERNATIONAL

ST Media Group International Inc.
11262 Cornell Park Drive. | Cincinnati, Ohio 45242

p: 1.800.925.1110 or 513.421.2050
f: 513.421.5144 or 513.744.6999
e: books@stmediagroup.com
www.bookstore.stmediagroup.com (ST Books)
www.vmsd.com (*VMSD* Magazine)
www.irdconline.com (International Retail Design Conference)